Hot Mess to
Not Mess

Kick the *Mindset* of Indecision &
Disorganization to the Curb
#FindFreedom

Dana Reed Nuesca

Hot Mess to Not Mess

Kick the *Mindset* of Indecision and Disorganization to the Curb #FindFreedom

Copyright © 2021 by Dana Reed Nuesca

Cover design by: SpeakTruth Media Group LLC

Cover photo: Marcy Browe Photography

Published by: SpeakTruth Media Group LLC www.speaktruthmedia.com

For information about special discounts available for bulk purchases, sales promotions, fundraising, and educational needs, contact by email: SpeakTruth Media Group LLC at order@speaktruthmedia.com.

ISBN (pb) 978-1-7364520-5-9
ISBN (eb) 978-1-7364520-6-6

Printed in the USA, First Edition

Dedication

To everyone who has followed my journey, mess and all!

To my Mom, Marsha, Dad, Wes, and Stepmom, Sharon. Your lives may have been a hot mess, but you taught me all I know. I am so thankful for each one of you!

To my husband, Kalani, who loves processes and procedures, despises change *and* is organized. I am the exact opposite! On the contrary, I am a fly-by-the-seat-of-my-pants, live life on the edge, no-gas-in-the-tank kind of girl, which drives him crazy. He has overcome much frustration in our 38-year relationship, 35 of those married. I am thankful you stuck with me through the highs (bumping your head on cabinet doors and lows (my obsession with pillows and you finding a way of tripping over them. You are my biggest supporter, cheerleader, and "*not-mess*" coach.

To my son and his wife, Aaron and Robin! I've been blessed with five amazing grand kids, Elizabeth, Asher, Elaina, Zayne, and Kainoa, three biological and two by the grace of God blending my family with another. I love them all so much.

I pray those "*grands*" get the "*uber-organized gene*" since I have to work so hard for it.

Finally, in memory of my dad, Charles Wesley Reed, who died on August 26, 2021. I'm so thankful he got to read my book and offer feedback before he graduated to heaven.

A verse in the Bible sums it up perfectly;

> "*And me? I'm a mess. I'm nothing and have nothing: make something of me. You can do it; you've got what it takes - but God, don't put it off.*"
> Psalm 40:17, The Message

...and that He did.

Contents

FOREWORD:
Who Needs This Book?

Women who feel out of sorts, out of place, who don't fit the traditional image of what is deemed a Christian woman or, in other words: wife, mother, friend, a church day laborer who might be relegated to the nursery instead of the pulpit, you need this book. I could go on and on! I am her, and I have overcome.

For years I felt stuck like I was in the wrong body. Thank God when I was struggling with this idea, gender choice was not an option. The enemy would have hoodwinked me into believing that I was born in the wrong gender, era, etc. I am where I need to be, and guess what? SO ARE YOU!

This book will break the mold of what a godly Proverbs 31 woman looks like in real life. She looks just like you. She may not cook or clean the best, but she raises a family and brings home the bacon. She may be a great listening ear, changing the world one person at a time while dirty laundry is growing by leaps and bounds in her home. As you follow me through my journey, you will see all that God has for you!

Join me now through the phases of my life as I went from *Hot Mess to Not Mess!* While I still find lingering moments of *hot mess*, I have discovered so much about myself and how I react to certain people and situations, that either perpetuates the *hot mess* moments or alleviates them, thereby catapulting me into a *not mess* state of being.

Friends, we will never arrive to a continual state of *not mess*, but we can grow as we learn how to deal with our *hot mess*. And, that is what matters most.

I love this quote:

> *"Right or wrong, make a decision. The world is paved with flat squirrels who couldn't make up their mind."* — Anonymous

Oh, and by the way, my name is not pronounced the traditional "Dana" way. *It's Dana-banana!* Now that we're friends for life, let's dive in, face first!

Phase 1

Hot Mess — My Story

I'm a 5th generation Californian raised in the Central Valley of California, which is a bit like being a Unicorn.

I was born to militant organizers: Mom, Dad, and Stepmom. On the other hand, I was not born with the organization/Martha Stewart/Marie Kondo/insert-any-organizer's-name gene. Don't get me wrong, I LOVE A CLEAN and TIDY house, office, and car, but it takes extra headspace and the need to slow down to get me to those places. I thrive in cleanliness, but it is a slippery slope for me that takes me to the abyss of clutter, ultimately leading to major disorganization.

My parents' motto (all of them) is "Everything has a place, and there is a place for everything." What happens when you don't care to find those places? You see, I flew out of the womb an extrovert, saying, "I am here! I'm ready to GO!" I had a high need for people and hated missing out on anything. As a small child, I remember wanting to be in the mix of everything. Putting something in its place often required me to remove myself from the goings-on around me. I would rather shove everything under the bed or in my closet and play outside all day. I had forts to rule, clubs to create, paths to ride. I was the neighborhood social director, calendar planner, and leader. My mom stayed on me to no avail. I was fast as lightning when it came to cleaning. Carrying this into my adult life was a catastrophe because I soon learned that the comparison game I played with various people on the other end of an imaginary measuring stick was ten times worse than being disorganized.

As a child of a divorced family with both parents being polar opposites except in the organization category, I may not have been the most organized. Still, I could make a decision like no other (more on that later). I would bounce back and forth between households. My dad's home was slightly bigger than the two-bedroom home I grew up in with my mom and sister. They had a formal living room that children dare not wander into for fear of leaving precious footprints on the newly vacuumed carpet. My stepmom had the patience of a saint as she parented four little girls: two of her own plus me and my sister. No less than thirty-two times a day, I would hear her say, "Please walk in the house. Stop spinning on the barstools. Who drank all the milk? We pick up our messes when we are done." And, Sharon, I was the milk drinker, gallons and gallons, confessing now since I didn't as a kid, but I know you knew the entire time. Side note, in first grade, I remember wishing milk came out of the water fountain. I had an affinity for it like no other. Today I am dairy-free! Who would have thought that possible?

Speaking of the back and forth between homes, my mom was a product of the hippy generation. She worked as a secretary for a local state senator during the week (uber professional) and let her hair down, packed up her VW camping van, and headed to the campground on the weekends. She was all about peace, love, tranquility, and throw in a bit of Marijuana to help her get there faster. If you've ever been around someone who smokes pot religiously, you know that laughter often ensues at your expense, and decisions are rarely made. My mom may be organized, but she was late for everything.

One such camping trip into the woods of Northern California proved that I could make grown-up decisions when faced with fear. The adults were all partying at the house near the river. The kids, me in particular, were bored and wanted to head out on an adventure. As a seven-year-old, I packed a healthy lunch full of Reese's bars and chips. I grabbed my friends, a brother and a sister, the same age as my sister and me. As the oldest sibling, I led the way. We walked down a path and found a raging river. Yes, this would be child abuse and neglect in the present day, but it wasn't back then. We ate all of our sweet/salty treats, told crazy stories about wild boar, almost scaring ourselves to death, but we somehow managed to stay clear of the roaring river. It was quite a feat since water is an attraction for young children.

We then decided it was time to head home as the sun was starting its descent. We quickly realized that we forgot where the path was. We screamed and yelled for help to no avail. We could no longer hear the Doobie Brothers blaring from the house. We were lost. Honestly, it feels like yesterday. The memory is so vivid. My friend took her brother and forged a different path. My little sister and I were crying, but I was consoling her as I had done so many times in the past, letting her know we would find the way. I would not give up. A few minutes into the pursuit of finding the path, I realized I was standing right on it. I grabbed my sister's tiny little hand and ran up the steep mountain. It could have been a small hill, but when you are little, it feels like Mount Everest.

It was then I realized I am a decision-maker. I would continue to make adult-sized decisions for the remainder of my childhood years. I was being trained, albeit not the way you want to be, but I learned to hone the skills that would make me who I am today. For that, I am so thankful. The school of hard knocks was indeed the best training. I could have given up and become a victim, but I decided life was worth fighting for, worth living.

Back to cleaning as a kid, I didn't learn my lessons even though I haphazardly made attempts at cleaning and organizing. Of course, I made my bed every day (per mom's requirement for living under her roof). The pattern was laid, and the damage was done. I started married life with a strong desire to get it right. Organized the kitchen, made the bed, folded the clothes, but that was short-lived. I began working, and we started a family. It was all I could do to keep up. Believe me, when a neighbor stopped by (like they did in the 80s), they had no idea the mess that was in my head and behind all those closet doors/kitchen drawers. My house always looked put together but was a total junk drawer when laid bare.

The pressure to produce and conform was huge!

The other thing about my personality is that I love it when people are happy. Yes, I confess, I am a recovering people pleaser. Because of my need to be well-liked (I blame it on Michelle, the 5th-grade bully—more on that later), I've been able to maintain some semblance of organization in my almost 54 years on this planet. And I must say, I've had major breakthroughs! With the help of the Creator of the Universe, you know the one who spoke organization into existence, He has reminded me that I can be organized because He is organized. Still, I don't have to be religious/perfectionistic about it. That set me free. He told me I wasn't built to color in the lines. That would have really ticked off my 1st-grade teacher, Mrs. Peabody (she is long gone now). She told my mom I would amount to nothing in the art world—good thing I am not that fond of art. Cross that off my bucket list of to-dos. She said I needed to learn to color within the lines and that most first graders had mastered that already. Not me. I just wanted to chat with all my seatmates; coloring was a boring, one-person show. As you can see, I have childhood issues. Don't we all, though?

In 2014, I did the craziest thing, unimaginable for a wanna-be organized person; I purchased a home organizational systems company. It is laughable because, of course, organization has always been my weak link. Why not figure it out? That is what I did. I couldn't believe it. Organizational systems actually kept me "coloring" within the lines. Systems really do work. I've devoted an entire chapter to just that.

This book will detail several stories of my incredibly wonderful, disorganized life thus far and all the breakthroughs I've had amid the clutter. Some may not feel like it, even getting frustrated with me and my approach, but hang in there. At the end of the book, you will be able to hold your head high and stay organized.

You've got this; we've got this! Stay tuned.

Phase 2

She Did WHAT?

Around my 11th birthday, my mom announced, "Girls, we are moving to Maui." I had no idea what she was talking about. I'd never flown in a plane, let alone traveled outside of CA. It was only going to be for six months. Well, we stayed way beyond the allotted time frame, my mom 30 plus years.

Life was simple on Maui. The perfect place for an extroverted kid. I could play outside all day, every day. Even when I was sick, a prescription of sand and sea was a must. I lived an isolated, fairly idyllic life. Homes and cars were not important; they were just items used to survive. None of my friends were rich, but we all had so much fun. Life was rich. It was on Maui that I would meet my husband. We are a high school sweethearts success story, and I know there aren't many of those anymore.

Three weeks before my 19th birthday, I married the man of my dreams. He joined the Marine Corps, and we ended up in a place far away from THE paradise I was used to, North Carolina, where I traded pidgin English for a Southern twang. Life was very different, and I felt much more segregated than my simple life in Hawaii. Don't get me wrong, as a haole (white girl-part Portuguese) growing up on Maui, I was not always well-liked, but I seemed to fit in there much better than with the Michelle's of the world (my 4th-grade bully, whose story is coming soon).

I moved to North Carolina several months after we married. I made my husband PROMISE he would not rent a mobile home for us to live in during that time. Right before leaving Hawaii, an article made it into our local paper about a tornado that ravaged a small southern town, taking out an entire trailer park. I wanted nothing to do with that. He reassured me repeatedly and even on the drive to our new home from the airport that trailer living was not in my future. Boom, we pulled up in front of a trailer, not just any trailer but a really old, small, rusted-out trailer. Bonus, the trailer was fully furnished to include a couch that looked like a scene out of the wild, wild West with wagon wheel pictures all over it and covered in a poly-velour, making it not only uncomfortable but hotter than hades to sit on. The bed must have been there over 100 years because the dip in the middle was so deep that once in, it was impossible to get out. Couldn't we afford a new mattress? We were newly married with barely a penny to rub together. Oh, the good ole days. My new digs sunk me right into further disorganization.

Side note about the trip to NC: back in the day before TSA was a thing, I bought an airline ticket from a newspaper ad off a girl named Terry, who had purchased a round trip ticket to Maui but decided to stay. Her ticket got me from Hawaii to California, and then I had to buy the final leg to North Carolina in my own name. The biggest bummer was that I couldn't check my luggage all the way through. I had to pick it up and recheck it once in CA. Here is where I made a foolish, 19-year-old move. I decided that I wanted to dress up for the 16-hour journey. I went to the local teeny bopper store in the mall, purchased an adorable yellow dress, and then walked over to the el cheapo shoe store to look for that perfect pair of white, high-heeled shoes. First of all, I had only worn high heels for a hot minute before this purchase. I was used to "slippahs" (flip flops for you mainlanders). I failed to see the error of my ways, as I wanted to look the "nines" for the reunion with my new husband, who would be waiting on the other end. I looked like I belonged in a freak show by the final leg, on a small puddle jumper plane.

I cried my eyes out from Hawaii to California because I had never been away from my mom for long periods. Halfway across the US, my stomach started to hurt because I was sad and excited all at the same time. With a window seat and multiple trips to the lavatory, I think my seatmate was ready to strangle me by the end of the second leg.

You've heard of that awful movie that still creeps me out called *Snakes on a Plane* ? How about "Sharting on a Plane"? Nope, because I am sure it has only happened to me. If you are unsure of the definition of "shart[2]," then you've been living in the 20th century. The dictionary (vulgar as it is defines it when "you expel feces accidentally when breaking wind. "Oh yes, I did. Again, I excused myself with my seatmate and proceeded to run down the aisle to the bathroom one more time. Now in a complete frenzy wishing I had packed all the "extras" my mom told me to pack, I was melting down right in the bathroom, which is hard to do on an airplane and rather disgusting, to say the least. When I finally landed, I fell into my husband's arms (who was so EXCITED to see me and cried my heart out. I was spent and looked as cheap as a $1 bill versus the $100 bill I was gunning for originally. I learned a valuable lesson that day; take the time to pack for emergencies. I've flown too many times to count now, and I can honestly say I am always prepared for anything.

By the way, it was in that trailer I learned that I didn't know a thing about cooking. The rusty water was no big deal according to the landlord, mold grows fast on a bathroom floor, and mice like to live in dresser drawers, especially on a cold Saturday night when the propane tank runs dry and can't be refilled until Monday. I also conceived the only child we would be gifted, probably in the mattress built for two but only really allowed one. Precious memories and lifelong lessons were learned through living there. I wouldn't change a thing. I began to discover that I was a supreme decision-maker and not as disorganized as I thought.

It indeed was the beginning of peeling the onion of my crazy life. You see, I ran away from Hawaii, hoping to find peace. Right after my 18th birthday, I received the curse of anxiety while sitting in a church of all places. I knew then I must be a horrible person to encounter fear during a God moment! BUT God is gracious and knew that very episode, although I felt chained, would be the same thing that set me free. I just had to go through a season of anxiety. Thank God I wasn't stuck in the TV show, *Who Wants to Be a Millionaire,* where you only get one lifeline. I needed many moment by moment!

I've had many "She did what/that" *hot mess* moments in my life. Each one has taught me that I am an overcomer, *not mess*, I've been equipped for such a life as this, and I will be for every moment. We can handle random "She did what?" moments, but what about the random moments that happen in front of a crowd? Now I know we can handle those too. It is all about perspective and perception.

Phase 3

Cleanup on Aisle Two: You Matter

We all have been in a grocery store and heard the familiar intercom lackluster voice say, "Clean up on aisle two." As if it was the 100th time said that day. Clearly annoyed with whomever was the cause of a case of water, laundry detergent, fill in the blank, spilling all over the floor. Many of us have been on aisle 2 when that is so rudely expressed for the whole store to hear. Guess what happens? I might be on aisle 10, but suddenly I have a Gladys Kravitz (Bewitched character for those not old enough to remember) moment and feel compelled to run over and inspect what happened.

I don't know about you, but I've had several of those moments throughout my life where I wish I could melt into the floor instead of dealing with the mess I just created. And to be honest, I am always glad when I am in the grocery store, and I am not the one to blame for the spill on aisle 2. I hate being perceived as an idiot, fumbling fool, or klutz, but the more I focus on avoiding those labels, the more I am perceived that way. Or am I?

In light of that, let's go back to grade school, shall we? Remember, in the first chapter, when I mentioned Michelle, the bully? I was born with a small mouth and large teeth. As a child, those large teeth were quite a sight. As a very awkward 4th grader, I was standing in the bathroom when Michelle, the most popular 5th grader, walked in with her entourage of girls wanting to be just like her. I was an immediate and easy target. She took one look at me and said, "You have the biggest buck teeth I have ever seen." I stood there in shock. Why would someone pick on me? I had done nothing. I didn't understand bullying at the time. I knew I had big teeth, but I had not developed a complex yet. To be honest, I didn't realize they were a problem until Michelle pointed them out.

I can still feel the emotions of that day and how I felt when I went home and looked in the mirror. She was right. I did have huge buck teeth. I sat in front of the TV, pushing my teeth in, hoping they would not stick out. My mom was a single parent, and braces were not in the cards for me. I had to do something. I repeated this pushing behavior over and over, night after night, and slowly but surely, my teeth began to straighten themselves out. I never did speak to Michelle again, but I set out to prove that my teeth could be fixed. Little did she know, as most bullies don't realize, her remarks had a life-altering effect on me. At that point, I realized I felt I wasn't very pretty, I wasn't going to be the popular girl, and I would have to fight to get others to like me, or so I thought. Bring on people-pleasing 101.

Cleanup on aisle 2 is something I avoided most of my life. I NEVER wanted to be that person, leaving a mess behind for others to clean. I've worked hard at pleasing others. How in the world does this have anything to do with disorganization and indecision? We are getting there.

When you begin to dismiss your own needs, worrying about what others think, disorganization and indecision set in, even in the small stuff. For example, my purse was always a hot mess, and still is. I won't take the time to put everything in its place because I don't want to inconvenience anyone. If I give the cashier cash at the grocery store, I will throw the change into my purse so as not to hold up the line, which is well and good, but then I can't find a single thing in my purse. I get out of the car, can't find my keys, while a vehicle is waiting for my spot. At some point, someone will have to wait due to my inability to stay organized.

In the past, every drawer in my house looked like someone broke in and was rifling through them, and my car, we won't go there. I call it the game of moving the piles around. Move them from one counter to another, one room to another, one closet to another, but never really tackling the issue of disorganization.

Here is the deal, I was only motivated to tackle it because of what others thought. Not because I wanted it done.

By the age of 25, I was engulfed in anxiety. Counseling was a bad word, so I did it sneakily because I didn't want anyone to know that I was out of control in my head. I couldn't drive far distances. Thank God we lived on Oahu at the time because driving a far distance was about 10 miles max. My husband was also in the Marine Corps but deployed most of the intense years of my anxiety-filled life. Way to go there, Hubs, leave me during one of my most challenging times. Just kidding, but it was God's way of healing me. I wasn't able to hide behind anyone. I was fully exposed, and God knew that is what I needed. He was right. Once I tackled the severe anxiety, I was ready to tackle the world.

I was born for more than worrying about cleanup on aisle 2. Who cares! Accidents happen. I needed to be free from the fear of spilled milk, poopy diapers running over while in public, throw up all over me and the poor customer behind me in the bank line. Yes, thanks to my newborn son and his one moment of projectile vomiting, I never wanted to revisit a bank. That is how it starts! We fear what others will think of us, and before we know it, we are crippled and can't leave home. Now with the invention of shopping online for everything, we never need to leave home. It was the mid-1980s and I didn't have the luxury of online shopping, because Al Gore had not invented the internet yet. We can live our anxiety-filled lives in secret nowadays, scrolling through social media wishing we had other people's lives. That does not have to be you! Life is meant to be lived and lived out loud with others. If I can do it, you can too. Messes happen, but they can all be cleaned up.

As you will see, I still have hot mess moments, but I don't live a hot mess life any longer. I've moved to the other side of *not mess*. Why? Because I don't fret when I am in a *hot mess* moment. I pray about it, fix it, and move on. I leave perceptions (which most of the time are mine) at the curb. I am who I am, hair on fire and all.

Phase 4

Hair on Fire –

Exploring Motives

Have you ever had those days where nothing goes right, and everything is CRAZY? Yep, my husband calls them my "hair-on-fire-days." My husband's last duty station in the Marine Corps was with the Presidential helicopter squadron in Quantico, VA, which was the pinnacle of his career. Not only had he arrived, but I had too. For those unfamiliar with military life, wives back in the day wore their husbands' rank like it was their own. I knew this last four years would be full of pomp and circumstance. We, as wives and Marines, had to be always on our best behavior. We were serving the President of the United States.

We arrived three days before 9/11 hit. I hadn't even received my overseas household goods, so I didn't have a TV and had no idea the world was falling apart around me. I got a phone call from a friend in Japan telling me that the Twin Towers got hit. I immediately grabbed a radio and started listening. Not more than a few minutes later, the Pentagon was struck. I couldn't believe it. We had just checked in to our new duty station, and already the world was in chaos.

Our first Christmas in the squadron led to a White House invite for a Christmas cookie affair almost canceled because of 9/11. We would dress up and be ushered through the hall of trees and into a formal dining room for cookies. Of course, the President was not there, but it was a token day, allowing the "commoners" a chance at walking the halls of greatness, and I was excited to grace those halls with my presence.

About a week before this special event, we decided to adopt a puppy from the humane society. We picked out the cutest puppy ever, bright red (Hound dog mix) and oh so sweet, or so we thought. She turned out to be a devil in disguise. She didn't like alpha women, like ME. She took longer than average to potty train. I wasn't raised with dogs, but my husband had a gaggle of dogs, all named Fifi. It made it easy to remember. But, I was out of my element trying to train this dog.

We had to be in DC at around 11:30 am. If anyone has lived outside of DC for any length of time, you know that you need to leave two hours early to get to your destination, which was only 45-50 miles from our home. One minor hiccup and it is complete gridlock on the freeway. My husband and I drove separately as he had to report to work after the cookie gala. He was not thrilled about the event, but I was in my element. I couldn't wait to walk the halls of the White House, and I didn't want to be late.

Since the dog wasn't potty trained, I put the dog in the garage, got in the car, and remembered I forgot to put my lipstick on. My husband's car was parked directly behind mine in the driveway, which was at an incline. As I was reaching for the sun visor, I had this crazy thought, "What if I hit the garage door opener and open the garage, and the dog gets out?" You can only imagine what happened next. I accidentally hit that button but quickly hit it again to close it. Our small puppy was too fast and out under the door in a hot second. I jumped out of my car, not realizing that I had placed the vehicle in reverse. As I jumped out with the door wide open (in a dress, mind you), my car starts heading down the driveway, right for my husband's car. I manage to jump back in and throw it in park, which was quite a feat in my high heels. My husband tears out of the driveway right at that time, oblivious about what is taking place. Then he sees my unmanned car and the puppy running hither and yon.

We are both out of the cars, chasing a puppy in my dress and my husband in his suit. The puppy doesn't know its name yet, so she can't be corralled. Finally, we grab her halfway down the block. My husband murmuring and complaining and asking me why in the world my hair was on fire? I don't have an answer, but I began laughing hysterically in my normal fashion, which perturbed him even more. We made it to the event intact, but my husband's frustrations were running high, and my husband almost abandoned the entire trip.

Side note: my second trip to the White House was not quite as eventful but equally frustrating. My husband was retiring from the Marine Corps and his military service to President Bush (Junior). We were to have a "grip and grin," a handshake and formal picture in the Oval Office with the President of the United States. I, once again, donned a pretty floral dress and was ready to meet our President. As we were waiting in the hallway outside the Oval Office, I could hear a gentleman announcing our names and then President Bush repeating those names, followed by a very personal question. Kalani and I stepped up to the doorway, our names were announced, and I couldn't believe my ears. President Bush said, "Welcome Eugene (my husband's given name) and Dana (pronunciation on point)." I was so caught off guard that I stood next to him, the photographer snapped the one and only picture, and I had my eyes completely closed, never to take that shot again. When the formal portrait arrived, I was devastated to see that I'd missed the whole picture and then noticed my dress was a duplicate of the curtains in the background. It was not my greatest stand-out moment for sure.

Does anyone else have hair-on-fire moments like mine? I do hope someone reading this understands. I've had more than my fair share of these moments throughout life, and being married to a conscientious engineer type has been rough for both of us. In almost 35 years of marriage, we may never fully understand one another, and our motives will remain misunderstood. Motive is defined in Google dictionary as "*a reason for doing something, especially one that is hidden or not obvious. Something that causes a person to act in a certain way, do a certain thing, etc.; incentive. the goal or object of a person's actions.*" In the story above, my husband truly believed that I intended to make him crazy. Believe me that is the last thing I wanted to have happen to him. I call him my grumpy, crunchy pants, a term of endearment, but not the side of him I like to see often. My intention is to get it right the first time, but that is not always how it looks, not only to him but also to those around me.

The greatest loss of relationship, whether marriage or friendship, is often based on what we perceived as motive or intentions. We all interpret things differently and often read into someone else's motives based on the lens we are wearing. While writing this book, I mentioned the car-dog story to my husband, and it unearthed emotions in him I thought were gone, but now I see only dormant. We talked about my motives. Although he knows it was a mistake, he can't begin to understand why it happened. He doesn't do three things at once like I have the levity to do (or clearly not do). I don't do it well, but I sure will try.

Here is another way of looking at it. When you come home from the grocery store and have 11 bags, knowing you can only carry five, but somehow you figure out how to carry them all in at the same time, that is me! I only want to make one trip. Inevitably, I end up dropping something along the way, but I did it in one trip and felt accomplished. People like my husband have no grasp of this concept. He will only take what he can. He doesn't mind making multiple trips.

As my mentor, Ann McDonald, often says, "We need grace for the pace." We all have different strides. Mine is not necessarily better or even right, but who am I to judge how someone runs or endures their race. My goal in life is to rejoice and see that we all walk, run, skip, but hopefully not crawl, barely making it over the finish line. I want to see all recognize their God-given motivation to thrive and not just survive this life. I want to be an encourager, not questioning the motives of every person. Questioning every motive will suck the very life out of you because now you feel like everyone is against you somehow, when in fact, they are not even thinking about you.

I've been known to be an aggressive driver—not a road-rager—I like to get where I am going, fast! I recently purchased a new car with a supercharged turbo. The salesman at the dealership begged me to settle for standard turbo because it was all they had in stock. I was not willing, so I waited for the one I wanted. Recently, I picked up a cake and had it in the back of my car. I had to turn into a parking lot at a snail's pace so I wouldn't flip the whole cake over. The driver in the car behind me was perturbed and raced off around me once I was clear. The driver questioned my motives and felt like I was turning slowly on purpose to irk the heck out of them. He/she must have missed the "T" for "turbo" on the back of my car. Did he/she not realize that I always drive fast except when I have precious cargo onboard? How many times have I felt like someone is doing the same to me? Maybe they too have a cake on the back seat of their car.

Who am I to believe or question that they were trying to tick me off? They don't even know me. Judging wrong motives leads to destruction.

We live in a world filled with hate, almost always based on perceived motives. WHAT IF INSTEAD[2], we stopped the judgment and focused on what we absolutely know and not what we think happened? When in doubt, find out. Let's stop assuming we know what someone meant. Ask, seek transparency. Will people lie? Yes, but that is not on you. That is on them.

I've been accused more than once of being blunt. In my younger years, I was blunt *and* rude. Maturity does something to you. I didn't want to lose good friends because I was a know-it-all, so I decided to continue to be my transparent self only when asked my opinion. If there is a glaring fault, and I am blind to it, point it out. Nothing worse than a large piece of spinach or black pepper stuck in your teeth, and no one tells you. I want to be that kind of friend and have that kind of friend.

I am sure I will be prone to more hair-on-fire moments, but I will laugh at myself and others instead of passing judgment. We could all use a little more laughter in our world because laughter truly is the best medicine.

I have to admit, though; the hair-on-fire moments are even funnier when they occur in the church. You know those moments where all you can do is laugh at yourself? It's good to laugh at yourself; it helps us to see things differently. When those moments do happen, I like to call them "slip-showing moments."

Phase 5

Your Slip is Showing

Does anyone even remember what a slip is?

That thing that goes under your dress? I stayed with a millennial-aged friend while on a business trip several years back and realized I had forgotten my slip and needed to borrow her iron for all the wrinkled clothing in my suitcase. She looked at me as if I was from another planet. Her exact words, "What are people going to see under your skirt? Your two legs?" Her words struck me as truth! Wait, what?! I was raised to wear a slip, and now I was questioning why I ever wore one! And her second statement did not set me as free as the first. "No, I don't own an iron! I just throw it in the dryer and let the wrinkles fall out." Needless to say, I ran over to the local Target and bought an iron for my stay. I have an ironing area in my current custom dream closet and use it almost daily, but the slips are all gone—no slip is showing here.

Now for the cold, hard truth. Women's slips have been showing for as long as they have been wearing them. When I was young, it was an embarrassing moment, but now people wear bras in place of shirts, so anything goes. I can't believe I blushed over a slight slip show.

I do remember one such funny story. Thank God that is not my own. We were new to a church; we took our seat on the back row so we weren't noticed, and we could sneak out if it didn't go as planned. Halfway through the service, I heard the door to the far right open and looked over to see one of the leader's wives coming through the door. She was making a beeline to the front row. As she passed a couple of aisles over, I quickly realized she made a behemoth mistake. She accidentally tucked her skirt and slip into her nylons, so her entire rear end was showing in front of the congregation. She was not a small lady either. You could feel the tension in the room for all who noticed, probably about 75% of the congregation. I have no idea how she recovered or if she ever even knew. Surely, she felt the cold when sitting on the seat.

Would you have said anything to this woman? Or would you have ignored it, giggled, left the church all together over the faux pas? If it had happened in our current day and age, it would hit viral video status. I wish I could say I told her, but I had an excuse. I was new to the church and didn't want to be that person. Besides, it was the leadership's responsibility to tell her, right?

Passing the buck 101, someone else will do it. Make a decision; let someone know that their slip is showing, their fly is down, or they are dragging a mile of toilet paper behind them. Transparency in the last few years has been my motto. I've set out to remove the embarrassing moments from people's lives even when it causes me an embarrassment to say so.

Transparency is not popular. Social media has allowed us to disengage, showing only our best foot, never displaying the ugly side of life. We've moved away from confronting the issues in person. We've become keyboard warriors, hiding behind our computers, telling the world how they should act using pseudonyms so as not to reveal who we really are. I recently saw an article about two Hollywood stars married over six years, and one of them ended the relationship via text. Is that even possible? It is in the world we live in today.

How do we counteract this? In March of 2019, Kalani and I were on vacation with some dear friends when we got a call you never want to receive on vacation. My mother-in-law, Rodana, known as Dana (same pronunciation as mine), had fallen ill and had to be taken to the hospital, and the prognosis didn't look good. We often joke that my husband married his mom. She had some health issues, but nothing glaringly obvious. Kalani and I booked the soonest flight back to Maui. We were not prepared for what we saw. A once strong-willed, vibrant woman was barely cognizant of her surroundings. Kalani has six siblings, five sisters, and one brother, so the room was filled with people all the time.

For some reason, a few days into her stay, I was alone with her in the room. She was sleeping, so I was perusing Facebook when I saw a post that jarred me. A dear high school friend, Sean Hart, had died of a heart attack. I sat there dumbfounded. I couldn't believe he was gone. I cried and prayed for his family. His step-sister, Brandi, is a dear friend of mine (mentioned in Phase 6). I knew she would be heartbroken.

As I was praying, I heard the Lord drop an idea into my heart that I had no idea how to bring to fruition. Instead of memorializing people after they are gone, He wanted me to honor them while on earth. I responded with, "Okay, Lord, I am willing to try, but what does that look like?" Sean was one of those guys who would have loved to be honored, actually needed to be honored before he passed. I didn't want anyone else on my friend's list to pass without honor. I wrote all the names of those I knew and had a relationship with, and I dropped their name in a jar. I decided I would daily pull a name and write a paragraph about each person. I did one and then realized the time it would take was intense, so I started doing #DailyHonor videos, pulling a random name and spending two to three minutes talking about what they mean to me and the world. Little did I know the small impact it would have on those honored. It began to change the way I felt about social media. I saw it as a way to counteract the cancel culture happening around me. It was a way to talk about those who may not be known. It was a "slip showing" moment. I was calling out the greatness in those who may not even know how they are perceived. I still have over 100 names left to pull in my jar. Each time I get excited about who will be next.

I would challenge anyone reading this book to do the same. We need to be seen, and sharing someone's greatest attributes with the world allows them to be known and honored.

In a world where everything seems to matter, slips showing should not. I love this scripture from Hebrews 12:1 the AMPC: *"Therefore then, since we are surrounded by so great a cloud of witnesses [who have borne testimony to the Truth], let us strip off and throw aside every encumbrance (unnecessary weight) and that sin which so readily (deftly and cleverly) clings to and entangles us, and let us run with patient endurance and steady and active persistence the appointed course of the race that is set before us..."* When I read "strip off,"

I think of women casting their slips to the wind, embracing truth, and not fainting when your slip is tucked into your nylons. By the way, nylons have been replaced by Spanx, so kick all the "encumbrances" to the curb. Honor those around you, and it will go well with you, which is life, according to Dana! Flip the switch, friends.

Phase 6

The Flip Got Switched

When talking to a friend recently, she mentioned listening to a sermon about Flipping the Switch. Without missing a beat, she told me her "flip got switched." Suddenly, a mental picture popped into my head of my friend doing a gymnastic maneuver that went terribly wrong. I must have laughed for five minutes. I love how our brains do that. Flip everything around. I have friends named Patti and Randy, and more often than not, I flip it around to Ratti and Pandy. Or my friends Jana and Andy become Anna and Jandy. Does that happen to you? Once it happens, it is hard to un-do or un-hear it any other way.

I have to talk myself through saying it the correct way, literally. It's definitely a "flip got switched" moment.

In 1998, my husband was given orders to Okinawa, Japan. I love to travel; I love to move, and I couldn't have been more excited. At the time, we were living in North Carolina, and Japan is almost halfway around the world. The preparation was exhausting: passports, pack up, medical exams to make sure we were healthy, selling a house, saying goodbye to old friends. On the other end, we were assigned "sponsors" who help us understand the new culture, the surroundings, and how military life works in a foreign country.

By the way, our sponsors, Mike and PJ, were the best, and they were sponsoring two families arriving at the same time. A sponsor signs up in a voluntary capacity, and ours went above and beyond. They were both extremely organized. They laid out three or four days of activities, including what time they would pick us up each day. They were true to their word. I wish I could say the same when I was slotted to be a sponsor. I failed miserably and backed out at the last minute due to my disorganization and significant time constraints.

Mike and PJ picked us up from the airport at around 10 pm after a grueling 16+ hour plane ride, including layovers. I remember the ride to the base hotel being very confusing since the Japanese drive on the opposite side of the road. I chalked it up to being tired and knew I would get the hang of it quickly.

The following day, our sponsors arrived at 7:30 am to pick us up for breakfast. I remember thinking when they told us how early they would be there that they were crazy. We would need to sleep in due to jet lag. They reassured us that we would probably wake up at 2 am due to the time difference, and we would struggle to stay asleep. They gave us a fairly large food basket filled with all kinds of goodies to hold us over until they arrived. They were right! At 2 am, my eyes sprung open, and I couldn't fall back to sleep. By the time they arrived, we'd eaten everything in the basket and were ready for breakfast.

We drove a short distance to the base club to eat, and I felt so disoriented. Assuming exhaustion had set in, I ignored it. Days later, after sightseeing the entire island, I felt more unsure of our new home. My brain couldn't flip the driving pattern. I became afraid and slightly obsessed when we got on the road. I actually waited a month to get my driver's license. We had to take a test since the road rules were vastly different from the US. Each time I entered the car, I started this mental process: the line is on the right side of the vehicle, when turning watch for vehicles in both directions just in case another American is just as confused as I am and chooses the wrong path.

I am a GREAT and fairly skilled driver. I've never got a speeding ticket, although I have a lead foot. I have a sense about other cars all the time. And I have an abnormal GPS brain which means I never get lost. Definitely, one of my super powers, and it comes in handy when shuffling large groups through streets like New York (that is another story for another book). BUT on the Japanese road, I had met my match.

It took a good four months of coaching myself through a driving session that started when I walked to the car. You wouldn't believe how many times I jumped into the passenger seat thinking it was the driver's seat. That is common for anyone who switches driving direction, but for me, it took longer. I would hit the windshield wipers when I was trying to tap the turn signal. I was indeed a hot mess for several months.

And then it happened. My switch flipped. I began driving like the pro, channeling my inner Danica Patrick. I had a new sense of freedom. The Japanese are the kindest people in the world but the most aggressive behind the wheel. They will cut you off while bowing profusely. No horns are needed. As a matter of fact, it is rude in their culture. So what do you do when you are in a foreign country? There's an old phrase, "Do as the Romans do." Bring on the aggressive driving. I was actually born for it and had been unable to use my skill set because I would probably be a product of road rage. Not my own but someone else's since I love to bob and weave in traffic, oh and don't forget the most important element, speed.

Every time we left for the US, I would have to retrain my brain, now on both sides, because I had to return to Japan. I've come to realize that I am definitely not the sharpest tool in the shed. I process slightly slower than some.

I played competitive soccer for years. I am athletic but was always mediocre because my response time lags. I would receive a ball and want to think about my next move. While I am thinking, the opposing team is stealing, which happened more than I care remember. I loved it when I found myself in an open field, receiving the ball and then thinking. When my husband and I moved to indoor soccer, it really showed. "No time to think, just kick!" became my motto.

My brain, along with many others, needs to wait for the "flip to switch" or switch to flip. Does that mean we are inferior, stupid, or ignorant? Absolutely not. Some areas require a little more processing, like RAM in a computer, so to speak. Being married to someone whose switch only needs to be flipped when he is speaking has been tough; his only weakness is articulation, and he isn't even that bad at it. His reasoning skills are off the chart.

He is always logical, beyond smart, and requires a lot of patience on my part and his. He, of course, does not understand why my brain processes so slowly at times. I have tried for 30+ years to explain it. We are uniquely different, gifted, and perfectly matched even when we don't see it. Time to actually flip the switch! Let's do it the right way. And when it comes out backward, hit the reset button and start again. Have grace for those who also have to hit the reset. Honestly, we should all carry a reset button like the one that Staples sells – the "That was EASY" button!

Unfortunately, we've all been programmed to think and act alike. I blame our education system. If someone is too hyperactive, they are medicated. It really isn't a teacher's fault. He/She has to deal with 30+ kids sometimes, and if I were in his/her shoes, I would want robots too. I can hear myself screaming, "KIDS, LISTEN AND GET YOUR WORK DONE." Not very teacherly, which is why I am not in a classroom. I am not cut out to nurture and teach little kids. The funny thing is when I started college; I wanted to be a nurse until I realized I HATE needles and seeing blood, so that idea went out the window quickly. I switched to Elementary Education because I was married to a Marine and knew I would have a job each time we moved. I remember thinking more about summer vacations than actually teaching.

Not a sign of a good teacher! BUT the switch flipped when I took an entry-level Communications course (the dreaded public speaking) and flourished. I absolutely loved it. I remember asking my professor if I could major in public speaking and make a living. He said, "No, but you can major in Communications and will most likely end up in sales." DONE! Sign me up. Yes, I am an oddity of sorts since I love all things public speaking, whether it is an audience of 1 or 1000.

Maybe you've struggled with a "switched flip?" Recognize it might just be your greatest strength and your greatest weakness, all in the same package. Embrace it or kick it to the curb, depending on which it is. Are you in a dead-end job, clinging to dead-end friendships/relationships or hobbies? We all have God-sized dreams in our hearts, but we often fear pursuing them because of what others might think. Too much risk relationally or financially equals failure, so we abandon our dreams to stay in the fray. Writing this book has taken three times what it should have taken. Why? Because I feared failure. I loved the concept of talking about a book, but putting hands to a keyboard was more challenging than I ever imagined. BUT I pressed on and did it because women need to hear that we are all created uniquely. I can't say it enough. THERE IS NO ONE LIKE YOU/ME ON THE PLANET.

To be honest, it is so much easier blending in. Why? Because if I am known, I might be known for all the wrong reasons. I might be the next viral video, called a Karen, misunderstood, so I tuck tail and keep quiet. I blend in. Father, forgive me! You've given me a voice and one that is not afraid of the stage. I always have Jesus who loves me, whether I am viral for all the wrong reasons or not!

I've been writing this book during the Covid pandemic. I've had very strong opinions that have alienated me from friends on both sides of the issue, so what did I do? I clammed up and decided to keep my thoughts to myself. Unfortunately, many have done the same, and here we are more than a year later, still locked down in various parts of the country, schools not open for children and families who desperately need them to be available. And if they are open, the children have to social distance, wearing masks the entire day, which does nothing for the social needs. Even the parks closed for quite some time. It has been ludicrous! And yet, my voice has been silenced because I fear what others think. I fear loss of relationships with friends and even family. Is there a way to tactfully get my point across?

Yes, and my platform now is that this can never happen again. We've got to get back to life as we know it! I will not live in constant fear as I know that according to scripture, "You have decided the length of our lives. You know how many months we will live, and we are not given a minute longer" (Job 14:5 NLT). We have permission to live and live life abundantly! I don't want anyone at my funeral saying, "She was afraid of everything." In my 20's that would have been what they said, but not any longer. I will not fear. When I die, I hope they say, "She lived a full life, taking major risks, and trusting Jesus every step of the way."

As I wrap up this chapter, my parting words are: make a decision. You know that you have something burning in your heart to say or do. DO IT! Don't wait for approval because it may never come. Of course, listen to the Lord and His promptings, but the audience of one should be our only concern. He has written things on your heart to say and do. Rip off the Band-Aid and get it done.

Wherever the switch needs to flip, flip it and get your heart and mind set on God's course for your life. He will help you see things clearly and respond to them rightly.

One thing that can derail a flipped switch is gossip. I saw a recent quote that said, "A lot of problems in the world would disappear if we talked to each other instead of talk about each other." That's the absolute truth, and we need to start talking *to* one another again. So, let's tackle gossip. I wish I could say I have no idea what that is, but I can't, and you will see why in the next chapter.

Phase 7

Gossip Girl

I wish I could start this chapter off by stating that I am no longer a hot mess when it comes to gossiping, but that would be a bold-faced lie. Actually, while writing this book, this chapter came to life. At almost 54 years of age, the struggle is real. I felt so convicted about something I said about someone recently. I felt like a headline was written on my forehead for all to see that I was, in fact, "The Gossip Girl."

Why do we take part in the hot mess of gossip? According to an article on Health.com[1], *people spend about 52 minutes a day gossiping or talking about a person who isn't present.* We always assume that gossip has only negative connotations, but we could be talking positively about someone who is not present. Sign me up for that. I have definitely been caught gossiping. I love to talk about the strengths of others.

According to Mark Leary, Ph.D., at Duke University, who commented in the same article saying, "*They (gossipers) need to have as much information as possible about the people around them in order to know what various other people are like, who can and can't be trusted, who breaks group rules, who is friends with who, what other people's personalities and viewpoints are, and so on.*" Leary goes on to say, "*Gossip doesn't only teach us about the person who's the subject of the conversation, but also about the person doing the talking,*" which is so true. How often has someone been telling you something about someone else, and you may realize this person is not safe to tell your secrets to? I don't cut them off from friendship, but I am careful about what I tell them.

When I think of gossip, it is always a negative term. I must admit I was happy to see its positive side and can't wait until I am mostly there. I have a long way to go. Gossip sneaks up on me, and before I know it, I am telling a full-blown story that shouldn't be said. And if I am candid, I go in, knowing I am going to tell a story I shouldn't be telling.

Back to Gladys Kravitz, the nosey neighbor on Bewitched that I mentioned earlier in this book, as a kid, I lived for each episode and never liked Gladys. She annoyed me because she was always poking her nose where it shouldn't be. Fast forward to adulthood, and honestly, I've been no different. I didn't snoop around looking in windows, but I have peeked through the blinds a time or two, opened my windows when the neighbors are fighting.

I lived in base housing for many years. You didn't need television with all the drama going on in the neighborhood around us.

I was a Christian and kept my issues to myself. I didn't air my dirty laundry for the whole street to hear (before social media where you can now air your laundry online), but I indulged and listened. I had a stockpile of self-righteous ammo that I used to make myself feel better about who I was or wasn't, which went on for years. Slowly but surely, the Lord began to work on my heart. Pray for the neighbors instead of judging them.

Several years ago, I was sitting in a pastor's office with a friend. We were just chatting about everyday life. I don't recall the subject or when I made a horrible turn down a dark alley, but I heard words coming out of my mouth that were not even true. I remember it like it was yesterday (not the actual conversation, just its emotions). I not only gossiped about a topic, but I flat out lied about it. I weaved a good story. Both parties seemed to buy it hook, line, and sinker. After leaving the pastor's office that day, I got in my car by myself, and I heard so LOUDLY in my spirit, "You have to tell the truth!" I begged and pleaded. Couldn't I just ask for forgiveness with Jesus and move on? No, I needed to either go back in or call the pastor. Because I was so embarrassed, I couldn't face him. I was ready to leave the church and never look back. I sat in my car and made the phone call. I told him I made the whole story up to fit in. He was gracious and laughed it off. To me, it was no laughing matter. I was broken over it. The Lord is always spurring us on to greatness. That was one of those moments. I've been a very cautious storyteller because of it.

Fast forward to a few months ago; I was struck by the words coming out of my mouth. Proverbs 16:28 TPT, "A twisted person spreads rumors; a whispering gossip ruins good friendships." Ouch, I felt that one. First of all, I may be a hot mess, but I sure don't want to be called twisted. And yet that was how I felt: exposed, raw. I repented knowing that repentance means to turn and walk the other way, a new direction. I felt free, lighter than I had in years. But the cliff was only an inch from where I stood.

Just like that, I found myself justifying the gossip. Well, she/he needs prayer or needs comfort from the person I was telling. They need to be heard—story told. Truth be told, I needed to be heard, to vent. I can plot and plan like there is no tomorrow. Again, I wish I could say gossip is in the rearview mirror, but it is not. For me, it may be a daily battle. Is this the thorn in Paul's side? I doubt it, but in being transparent, it is mine, which makes me thankful for forgiveness. If you truly want to overcome something, hand it wholeheartedly to the Lord. I've been doing that daily since the revelation a few months back.

I woke up the other night, mid-dream, and knew that my words over someone had been detrimental to their life. I quickly repented and prayed a declarative, restorative word over this person. See, that is how to partner with the Lord. When you ask, He will show you. I am asking, so I know He will reveal all that is in my heart. I want nothing to stand between us.

Without doing further research and relying solely on the Lord for wisdom, I am going out on a limb to say that there are multiple reasons we gossip:

> #1 - We want to look better than others taking a self-righteous look at ourselves.

> #2 - We want to be seen in a world of the "unseens."

> #3 - We truly think we are doing it for the right reasons.

#4 - We love to be "in the know," telling things to others before it has been revealed.

I was explaining the last line to a group of women recently about my need to know things and not be left out. My mentor, Ann, made a bold statement about being in the know. She said, "Dana, you are called to know things. Begin listening to what He is saying, and you will know more than you can ever imagine." I was blown away. She is right. It was a positive spin on what I'd always deemed a negative perception of myself. When I feel like I've been left out or in need of knowing something, I stop and ask the Lord for clarification. I ask Him if something is missing that I need to know about that situation. He knows all things. If I am to know, He will tell me.

How do we avoid the age-old issue? Avoid being a gossip girl? Several years ago, as I mentioned throughout this book, my husband and I started a business. We have tremendous strengths but also have glaring weaknesses. Most people have a hard time focusing on strengths. It is so much easier to point out flaws. We feel if we focus on flaws, it will correct the weakness, but what it does is bring shame and anger. We feel attacked. My husband and I had no idea that it would almost tear apart our marriage. Unfortunately, I've gossiped to close friends about my frustrations with my husband and his idiosyncrasies in the last seven years because I couldn't call out his greatness. He couldn't see mine either. We are truly a match made in heaven but turned our lives into hell. We aren't there, but with help from many and lots of prayer, we are beginning to see that we were uniquely created to run together.

Proverbs 18:21, TPT, says, "*Your words are so powerful that they will kill or give life, and a talkative person will reap the consequences.*" The Amplified Classic reads, "*Death and life are in the power of the tongue, And those who love it and indulge it will eat its fruit and bear the consequences of their words.*" These words hit so close to home. I've been called a motor mouth, told I have been accused many times of using A LOT of words. Although I know I've been equipped to speak (my geatest gift), it is, as I've said prior, my greatest weakness.

To think that "life and death are in the power of the tongue." It must be the truth because God spoke the world into existence. Therefore, I need to guard what comes out of my mouth for the sake of myself and others. When I feel like cursing, I need to bless. When I feel like gossiping, I need to stay quiet and ask Him if I need to know something. When I feel inadequate, I need to exploit someone else's gifts and callings positively.

For many years, I felt that I couldn't compliment people, especially in public speaking arena, because then it would seem that I wasn't as good—total insecurity shining through. Over the years, I've begun to see that it actually builds me up in the process when I genuinely applaud someone for great work. I've learned to rejoice with those who are rejoicing, even when my same breakthrough has not entirely presented itself.

The gossip decision is not an easy one, but one that, if looked at through a different lens, can be tackled with the word of God and His reminder that our words create spiritual structures that become the physical structures we live in right now. For example, if you grow up being called a worry wart (as I was) through your formative years, you will physically manifest a fear. I didn't have my first anxiety attack until I was 18, but the damage had been done. I knew I was a worrywart; therefore, I deserved to be anxious. BUT GOD! He knew I was born to be fearless, so He rewrote my history in my mid-20s, calling me fearless instead of fearful. As a child, what should have been spoken to me was that I care about all the details. I care about who is where and what they are doing.

Look for the gold in others. As you begin digging, it will release the gold in you! Years ago, I was working in our church café after service. I ran the register, and my husband was the barista. All newcomers received a free latte card. An older gentleman came in towards the end of the café hour and presented his card, but what happened next changed my perspective on so many things in life.

I exchanged pleasantries with him. I felt like he was looking right through me. I had been freed from so many insecurities by that time, and I welcomed the gaze into my soul that he seemed to have. He began by asking me simple questions: how do you like working here? How long have you been doing this? You seem like a pro? How long have you and your husband been married (I told him the barista was none other than my husband)? And to be honest, I don't remember the other questions. But I felt like I was the most important person in the room. I should have been asking him those questions as he was brand new. He was from out of town visiting a family member.

I left that day knowing I was called to do the same. I am called to listen and ask the right questions and called to mine the gold in other's lives, and called to gossip about people the way God would. I am learning to master that trait, and I have worked very hard at listening to others versus thinking about what I am going to say the minute they are finished with their thought. I try to let a thought sit for a few seconds before I even respond. I was talking to my stepmom, Sharon—a true gem, just a couple of weeks ago, and she said that I am blessed because I listen well. Honestly, I was shocked. I've purposed to hone the skill, and it was amazing to hear that it was recognized.

NEVER fall for the lie or get stuck in a mindset or say, "It is just the way I am." I am living proof that we can change. Make the decision today to listen, call out, and call up those whom God has entrusted into your care. Mine for gold instead of trouncing a reputation. I promise you; your life will change. Your outlook will change. You will begin to see things from a different perspective. I dare you to try it! One day at a time.

The Gossip Girl who tears down is gone; the Gossip Girl who builds up is fully loosed today to be and give others all the good she has in her heart to give.

Now you are ready to GO!

Phase 8

Lash Out

My greatest strengths are my greatest weaknesses. I am an adept and skilled communicator, which means when I am in a *hot mess* moment, I communicate in ways that are below my heart level, more like a take-out-the-knee level. You will see me in full action when I am tired and hangry. But this is not about *that*.

When I was in high school, I was briefly on the swim team. I hated that every time I got out of the pool, I had mascara running down my face. Heaven forbid I *not* wear makeup before entering the pool. I discovered waterproof mascara that year in 9th grade, not realizing it would send me down a very rough and often depressing path for the remainder of my life, or at least until today.

I am sure you are wondering how in the world could waterproof mascara have that big of an impact on anyone? As many of you ladies know, it is very difficult to rid your eyes of the stuff without a ton of makeup remover. I did not use or desire to spend my money so "frivolously" when I had so many other things I wanted to buy with my minuscule allowance and babysitting money. To remove the mascara, I would pull it off my lashes, not realizing I was pulling my eyelashes out. What started as a simple solution for makeup removal turned into a lifetime habit called *trichotillomania*[4] which is the "recurrent pulling of one's hair. Hair pulling can occur in any region of the body in which hair grows."

What began as a simple way to remove makeup turned into a lifetime affair with OCD (obsessive-compulsive disorder). I've always been a Type A personality or "D" for dominant on the DiSC profile, which lends itself to perfectionism. It was the perfect recipe for disaster that would often leave me ashamed and withdrawn. As an extrovert, I would retreat in fear that someone would notice. And further, I am a Christian; I shouldn't have these issues.

One day in college, with a ton of eyeliner on trying to hide the fact that I had not an eyelash on my lid or any eyebrows, I was turned in my seat talking to another student. Out of the blue, she asked why I didn't have any eyelashes. She asked if I had a disorder. I felt naked and exposed. I wanted to cry. I tried to explain the issue, but in 1994 I knew little about trichotillomania, and Google didn't exist. I honestly thought I was the only one with this strange disorder.

At the height of my picking fest, I went on vacation with my mom, who hadn't seen me in a couple of years. She knew that I struggled with pulling my eyelashes, but even she didn't understand it. When we were reunited in 1997 at Disney World, "The Happiest Place On Earth," in Florida, the first thing she said was, "You are still picking out your eyelashes?" "Yep," was all I could manage to eke out—exposed again.

Finally, in 1998, I was standing in the kitchen with my husband and our very handsome, single neighbor, Chris, when he asked why I had Band-Aids all over my fingers. Before I could answer, my husband blurted out that I bite my fingernails and pull out my lashes and was trying to avoid doing both. I ran to my room, never to emerge, crying my eyes out. I couldn't believe my husband told a stranger my personal story, which I wanted never to reveal. My husband apologized profusely, but the damage was done. He said he had no idea what possessed him to betray my most secret addictions.

The next morning, I was out early walking the dog when a car approached from behind, startling me. It was Chris.

I shouted in my head, "NO!" I never wanted to see him again. He apologized for my embarrassment the day prior. Then he said something I never expected. He asked me if he could share something with me. He lifted a piece of hair on the side of his head, and he had a very large bald spot. I couldn't believe my eyes, someone who knew how I felt, who could empathize with my pain. He said he'd struggled with it for years but managed to keep it hidden with a creative haircut. The only person that really knew was his barber and now me. That day was a turning point. I knew there were others. I was not alone. I also knew that my husband's faux pas was truly the grace of God at work. He wanted me to see that I was not a freak. That even handsome neighbors struggled with hair pulling.

Honestly, I vowed that I would not be afraid to share my struggles from that day forward because it just might set someone else free. And share I have. For about the last ten years, I maintain a fairly healthy set of natural eyelashes. I have *hot mess* moments: when I am overly bored, overly excited, or overly worried. I no longer fret when it happens. There is regret, but not fret. With the invention of eyelash growth serums, it has been game-changing. What took months to grow now takes only a week.

If this chapter does anything, I hope it encourages you to be vulnerable and transparent. If you are hiding, come out and let others know your struggles. You may just set someone else free.

We all have "things" we wish would go away. I am not talking about moral failures, but those things that are true "thorns in our sides." I may walk through this life never overcoming trichotillomania, but it will not own me, keep me from interacting with others, and, *or* hiding in disgrace. I made the decision long ago to embrace the current state of my eyelash affairs; whether thick or thin, it does not define who I am. Although I must admit, long, natural eyelashes look one hundred times better. I work hard to keep them thick, but I give myself grace when they aren't.

Make the decision today to embrace the hard stuff, the stuff you would rather run from than embrace. It may be a *hot mess*, but you don't have to live there permanently.

Phase 9

To Decide or Not to Decide

I am a born decision-maker. Guess what? So are you!

I can hear you now: "You don't know me."

"You don't know that it takes me two years to decide on what kind of carpet I want in my house. As a matter of fact, by the time I've made my decision, the styles have completely changed."

"I am not married yet because I can't commit, and I am afraid I will make the wrong decision."

"I hate my job, but stay for fear that I won't be able to recognize my lifelong dream of being an entrepreneur."

"I can't decide what to buy at the grocery store, the clothing store, any store."

If you are reading this book, you are probably a believer in Christ, and if not, there will be an invite at the end of this book to do so because I will say the best *decision* you will ever make is putting your hand in His. You see, Jesus was perfect and born a decision-maker. He states that "He only does what He sees the Father doing." And if we invite Him in, then He lives in us. Take that in for a minute. He lives in us! Therefore, if He, who was/is perfect, lives in us, we, too, are decision-makers.

I honestly do not fret over decisions that need to be made. I know what trips me up, so I avoid those traps altogether. For example, there are several big-box clothing stores that I won't be caught dead in unless I am buying perfume, purses, and shoes. The clothing In those stores is situated so that someone with my personality type cannot wrap my mind around where to go when I just want a blouse.

Figure out what makes you productive, makes you tick, floats your boat, brings joy and life, and then stick with it! Don't get caught in the comparison trap, well, Sally can do it; why can't I? You are not Sally. You are wired differently. We spend so much of our lives feeling like we need to be like everyone else when, as I've stated before, there is no one like us. Comparison is an ugly game that you will always lose.

When I was in high school, I managed to become very close friends with one of the most popular girls, Tobi. We attended church together and became fast friends. I must say I loved being her friend. Her status got me into places and I became friends with people I may not have otherwise had without her. I also became the girl that all the guys wanted to talk to in those days. Why? Because they wanted to find out about her. We were at a dance, and one of the most popular guys came up and asked me to dance. "What in the world is going on?" I thought. As we were out dancing, he asked me if I could ask Tobi to dance on his behalf because he feared her rejection. He told me he really liked her. That was a killjoy for sure. I wanted to run off the dance floor and hang my head in embarrassment. But I also knew that this would be my life if I wanted to remain friends with her. Good thing she was and still is an amazing person. There was no question. The decision was made. I wasn't that finicky, and I loved her as a friend.

A year later, my future husband (I didn't know that at the time, of course) walked in my life when we were registering for 11th-grade classes in August of 1983. I'd had several classes with him the years prior and liked him, but he wasn't part of my friend group, and he wasn't popular at all. But something happened during the summer of 1983. He must have hit puberty because I couldn't believe the transformation when I saw him that hot (in more ways than one) August day. He was taller; his hair was lighter as he had been surfing all summer, and his physique had totally filled in. As I was standing in line with Brandi, I saw my future husband walk by and whispered to Brandi, "Wow, he is so good-looking." Brandi looked at me and sprinted towards him. Before I knew it, Brandi blabbed all that I had mentioned while waiting in line. I was mortified.

After registering for classes, he cautiously approached me and asked, "Will you go steady with me?" I laughed out loud and said, "How about we start with a football game? And are you just asking me because you want to get to Tobi?" He looked at me in total confusion. I told him all that had happened over the past two years and how everyone wanted to ask me out with the intention of asking Tobi out. He emphatically stated that in no way was that his intention. He had liked me for over a year. The "Tobi" curse was broken. I finally had someone who liked me for me.

Okay, there never was a curse, but in my mind, I wasn't equal with Tobi. I made up a ruler of measure in my mind; she was at one end, the popular end, and I was at the other—not-so-popular. I didn't have a grid for who I was at that age. People go through their entire lives wishing they were someone else, looking like someone else, have giftings like someone else. If you are reading this book, I want you to stop and ask yourself these questions:

1. Am I happy with who I am?
2. What is my thought life when thinking about myself?
3. Do I often wish I was someone else?
4. Why I am unhappy with me?

Friends, if you've read this far, then you are ready for change. You are ready to step into a decisive way of life, as you kick disorganized thoughts to the curb. The first step is to thank God for who He created you to be, knowing we all have "dimples" and "curves" physically, mentally, and spiritually. God is not asking for perfection. He knows you; He designed you. He is asking, "What is in your hand?" Your response should not be to recite what everyone else has in their hand. He is asking you. When you begin to believe that He *has* called you and *will* equip you, then you can answer the question of what is in your hand.

As I write this book, I am reading several books. I am a

voracious reader and love public speaking, but writing is tough for me. I want to be witty, funny, and even sarcastic, but guess what? I am not that way in real life. I am a truth-teller, butt-kicker, transparent speaker, and very plain Jane most of the time. So why in the world am I trying to be something I am not? Because I, too, get caught up in the comparison stream of life! It is time to turn the other way and swim the way God called me, not the way that everyone else is going.

I wrote this book, praying someone else will change directions and remember who He has called them to be! If you don't know, then ask. Maybe you need guidance from someone who can point you in the way you should go.

You can learn a lot about yourself by discovering what the patterns of your life reveal about you. And, regarding organization, there are several organizational types that, when defined, can help us find out who we are and where we are in our "hot mess to not mess" journey.

Read on to find out!

Phase 10

What is Your Type?

Since purchasing my organizational systems business, Tailored Living featuring Premier Garage, in San Diego, I've been asked to speak on the topic of organization to several women's groups. I've been invited into hundreds of homes, often into the most intimate part, the closet. There are three types of organized people in this world. I call them the Uber-Organizer, Wanna-Be Organizer, and Could-Care-Less-Organizer. So, which one are you?

The Uber Organizer

This book was not written for the Uber Organizers of this world, although I hope they pick it up. After all, they need to understand the plight of those who unfortunately did not receive the Midas touch of organization. They don't realize they were born with a gift to organize, to see everything in its proper place and nothing out of order. They often think people in the other categories are lazy and unable. We need you "Ubers"! We need you to share your gift with all of us. Recognize that your strength might be someone else's weakness. Marie Kondo and others have figured that out. They are sharing their gift with the world.

The Wanna-Be-Organizer

"Wanna-Be-Organizer" is where I would put 75% of the population according to the houses I've traipsed through and seen with my own eyes. These people LONG to be organized and can be, but life takes hold, and before they know it, stuff is everywhere. I've been in many garages and closets, finding myself in precarious positions trying to get accurate measurements. Laundry is piled high in the corners of their closets. Boxes and boxes of paraphernalia stacked on one another to the ceiling in the garage, so I can't get to the walls. It is a chronic problem. We have an affinity for acquiring stuff. With Amazon at our fingertips, we buy/consume items at a faster rate. Before we know it, we are overwhelmed, hoping that an organizational system will help. My first recommendation is always purging while preparing for systems to be installed.

We are the "pile people." Yes, I fall into this category. I will have the cleanest desk on the planet at any given moment, and five minutes later, I am growing paper piles that are out of control. Here is the deal; I've employed organizers in my life like people use counselors. I need a complete overhaul about once a year and a touch-up every six months. With the right systems in place, I can stay clutter-free. See the recommendations at the end of this chapter.

The Could-Care-Less-Organizer

On to the Could-Care-Less-Organizer, which is where I would love to live; to be honest when you show up at this person's home without notice, he/she flings the door open wide unapologetic about the mess that lies behind. They welcome you in with open arms as you trip over the dropped clothing near the front door. They invite you to sit at the table clearly being used as a laundry folding station with a few crumbs left over from the morning breakfast. Organization is not on their radar because they are free to be who they were created to be, just plain ole, no-excuse messy.

More on the Wanna-Be

Let's dive back into the Wanna-Be-Organizer for a few minutes since most of the population lives there. What motivates us to want to be an organizer but never measuring up to it in full? The answer is us; we must encourage ourselves. If we organize for others alone, we will never be satisfied. We will never measure up. We've got to get to the point where organizing and decision-making comes from a place of joy in us. It "sparks joy," as Marie Kondo says.

Whenever we transferred with the Marine Corps, I decorated the home the minute we moved in. I had a rule pictures must be hung within 48 hours of moving in because I needed normalcy. And I wanted to impress the busybody neighbors. In the military, the minute the moving truck pulled up, the neighbors were at your front door, sizing you up. How many kids do you have (I was an oddity with numero uno)? What rank is your husband (we were all similar since we lived in the same neighborhood)? What kind of furnishings did you bring (are you uppity or poor)? It was always a race to beat the neighbors before the first knock.

In one such location, which shall remain nameless, I met Jackie*. She, too, had one child at the time, around the same age as my son. We became fast friends. When you are stationed in one place for only three years, you make friends fast because they are quickly gone.

Jackie proved to be a formidable foe (really a friend). One day, still new into our relationship, I walked over to see if her daughter could come out to play with my son. Jackie answered the door dressed in full cleaning gear: apron, gloves, bucket. I didn't even own a pair of gloves and never had. I asked what she was doing, and she bluntly replied, "Today, I am wiping down all the baseboards in the house." At that moment, I had no earthly idea what she was talking about. What the heck are baseboards? I am sure I don't have them. I ran home to see, and sure enough, they were right there at the base of every wall and full of dust. My eyes were opened that day, and I knew I, too, needed to tackle the baseboards with ferocity. That was just the beginning of my downward spiral to becoming a Stepford Wife (Google it if you aren't familiar).

Next came my introduction to the wonders of Mop & Glo. Jackie's floors were bright and shiny. My floors needed to be the same, slipperier than a wet baby with lotion. My poor son constantly complained and slipped multiple times, but oh how they shined. And then there was an ugly side to Mop & Glo, it turns a nasty shade of yellow with numerous layers and needs to be removed, which requires hours of elbow grease, but hey, I am keeping up with the neighbor, right?

Here is the deal, Jackie was not the issue. All of that organizing and cleaning brought her joy. And I thought keeping up with her would do the same for me. It didn't. I was miserable. My son was frustrated, and my highly organized husband was deployed, so not there to enjoy my brilliant, beautiful, shiny floors and baseboards. I became someone else. I became a slave to my home. My son felt like he had to take all meals outside because, heaven forbid, he dropped something on the floor.

God has a way of making you laugh, though. Another neighbor had two small children. I hardly ever saw them, just their little ones. One day my son asked if Shayla* could come in and play in his room. By this time, I had arranged my son's room in "centers." He had a library, art, Legos, and toy section, and they never mixed. Shayla had other plans as a three-year-old and a product of a free-range household. A friend shared this term which means parents who have an anything goes type of home and parenting style. That was not how I ran my home. We had rules upon rules, slight overkill. Being that Shayla was not accustomed to rules, she decided to use the art area to paint the bottom of her feet orange and walk down my newly laid Mop & Glo hallway, onto my mauve carpet, and out the door. Horrified as I saw the footprints,

I fell on the floor in tears, yelled at my son that he should have been watching her, and she was never allowed in the home again.

You can never find joy when you live in someone else's shadow. I used Jackie as the ultimate measuring stick. She was at the "right" end, and I was clearly on the wrong end. I didn't come close to measuring up. I couldn't figure out how she found joy in cleaning. I also didn't realize she was an introvert and a one-person kind of friend. I was her only friend at the time and would be until they moved away. I remember making a vow that I would not find another friend like Jackie at the next stop. I needed freedom. The problem was I didn't realize the issue was in my own heart. Jackie never required a clean home as part of the equation for friendship. I just felt it was implied, imposed it on myself, and felt inadequate as a result.

We've all heard it said a million times: there is no one like you on the planet. I love a plaque I have that reads, "Don't try so hard to fit in when you were born to stand out." Why then do we want to look, act, and talk like others? Because we aren't secure in the mold we were made from by our Creator. We believe it to be flawed. We aren't smart, articulate, pretty, tall, short, skinny, fat, you fill in the blank, ENOUGH! ENOUGH is enough! We need to stop comparing ourselves to others. We make unwise decisions when we do. We become crippled with fear and can't clean our house because it won't look like Jackie's. So, we don't try at all, or we drive our families bat crazy trying to keep up with the neighbors.

I don't use Mop & Glo and stopped the minute Jackie moved away, but guess what? Part of my company does epoxy flooring, so my husband and I epoxied my entire downstairs to look like a Mop & Glo floor with little to no effort when cleaning. And it is slick as ice but great when running and sliding in your socks. I loved the look but didn't like the maintenance. Why? Because it took me away from spending time with precious people.

If you don't read anything else, I pray you read this: *your strengths are NOT someone else's, just as your weaknesses are not the same.* We all have something to bring to the table. We know that we can't all be the head. I remember our teacher telling us that we would go nowhere if everyone wanted to be the big toe. She is right. We all have a part to play, and we are uniquely gifted for that part. Stop judging others for the parts they have to play. Stop being envious, jealous, and angry. LIVE your life! And, don't live in someone else's shadow either.

No matter your organizational type, there is help. Yes, even the Uber Organized needs freedom from judging all those not quite like them. If you haven't picked up on it by now, we need one another. I love a few verses from The Passion Translation in 1 Corinthians 12:17— 20, *"Think of it this way. If the whole body were just an eyeball, how could it hear sounds? And if the whole body were just an ear, how could it smell different fragrances? But God has carefully designed each member and placed it in the body to function as he desires. A diversity is required, for if the body consisted of one single part, there wouldn't be a body at all! So now we see that there are many differing parts and functions, but one body. Let's rejoice in one another's strengths and cover weakness."*

I don't know about you, but we seem to live in a world that loves to exploit other's weaknesses. Do you find yourself rejoicing when someone is taken out or down? Why? Don't worry; it creeps into my heart too. It takes the focus off us and puts it on others. Our thoughts run something like, "I am not that bad. At least I didn't do that." And to some degree, we do this with organization. We are visiting someone who is a "Could-Care-Less Organizer," and suddenly, your organization points go through the roof. The conversation with your spouse on the way home goes something like this:

You, "Did you see how messy their house was?"

Spouse, "Sure did. They've always lived that way."

You, "So glad I am not THAT BAD."

Spouse, "Uh-huh"—as if to say, "Sure, honey."

We all have moments. Most people, when visiting my home, comment on the fact that it is always in order. It is as long as no one opens the doors and drawers in cabinets. I can't promise things won't pop out. Occasionally, a friend may stop by unannounced and you will find something out of place: dishes in the sink (my husband claims that I throw parties when I am by myself—lots of dishes), clothing on couches, on the floor, and mail everywhere, piles and piles of it. That is what I call my "hot mess" moments. I embrace it when I am in those seasons and then quickly get it turned around.

As I've said earlier, when I can't quite get it turned around, I seek professional help by bringing in the professional organizer. Nothing wrong with surrounding yourself with people whose strengths are not your own. I know who I am and my capabilities, and I quickly recognize when things are beyond my giftings.

Here are a few practical tips and tricks to keep the clutter at bay and keep you sane:

1. Purge anything not worn for over a year. Chances are you won't wear it again. Ask yourself out loud why you haven't. You will find there is an answer.

2. When you buy a new shirt/pants/shoes, rid yourself of at least one item in the same category.

3. Hangers in the closet should all be one texture and color. I prefer black velvet because they are non-descript. Our brains process information at alarming rates. If you have pink, white, yellow, and wire hangers, your brain begins cataloging all those colors when looking for that purple shirt. If you opt for one type of hanger, your brain will bypass that information, and you will find that purple shirt quickly. Our brains love consistency.

4. Have a shred pile in an area near where you bring in the mail. I wish I could say I shred religiously, but it usually piles up. I have a granddaughter whom I pay to shred all my documents. Totally worth it, and she loves the extra money.

5. Invest in an organizational system. You won't be disappointed. It has changed everything for me.

You see, with organizational types, we all need to make adjustments, and those adjustments will ultimately bring us joy. Try a few of my tips and let me know.

Phase 11

All Systems Go

Embrace the life that Christ has laid out and ordained just for you! Even when you make a mistake, learn and most definitely laugh. A few years ago, my husband and I purchased a Groupon kayaking trip in the La Jolla cove. We were so excited. We met up with about ten other couples, whom we did not know, and we're ready to roll. As we got to the beach, our amazing tour guide asked who was an experienced kayak enthusiast. My husband and I shot up our hands as a definitive: US! He told us to grab our kayak and meet the group beyond the waves at buoys. He was going to give a brief class.

We grabbed our kayak, excited that we were the only experienced couple in the group. We are from Hawaii and have kayaked there several times. We had this in the bag. As soon as my feet touched the water, I quickly realized I wasn't ready for the cold. The day was also overcast, so I really wasn't ready to get wet. One thing you have to know about me: I may not get hangry, but I hate being cold, so I can be insensitive and rude when faced with freezing "anything."

I quickly announced to my husband that I was jumping in the kayak, and he would need to get us out beyond the waves quickly. I am that wife, queen for a day. He worked and worked, and the waves slammed the front of our kayak. Each wave brought a wet blanket of water over the top of me. I yelled in my Cruella Deville voice, "Get this kayak out to the buoy." He yelled back, "I am trying. If you would get out and help, we would get out there faster." Um no. I don't want to get wet even though I was currently drenched.

The next wave rolled our kayak. I emerged from the water as if I was Triton of the Sea. I was ready for battle. I wanted blood. We quickly right-sided the kayak and began to paddle like we'd just seen a great white shark. My sidebar comments about our inability to work this kayak were not helping. While paddling, Kalani kept repeating that something was wrong with his seat. I emphatically stated, "Nothing is wrong. Paddle faster instead of figuring out your seat."

We made it to the buoy. Safe at last, but now we were both pretty angry. The other couples were quickly behind us, nice and dry. The tour guide, a young surfer dude, pulled up next to us and said, "That was an epic entrance. You managed the waves well, including the roll. When you get a chance, hop out of your kayak because you are in backward." At that point, I was mortified. I couldn't believe, we the experienced ones, had made such a grave mistake. We were so mad at one another, but we've since been able to laugh out loud about the entire situation. We embraced the fact that we didn't have it all together, the *hot mess* kayaking trip has turned into a wonderful memory. Did that stop us from pursuing other exploits? Absolutely not. All systems go for us all the time. We learn and often laugh wildly about our failures.

We are almost to the end of this book. If you've learned anything, I hope that you finish reading knowing that you are uniquely made. Comparison is a game of risk and not worth playing. You never win because you never fit the person's status quo on the other end of your yardstick. Whether it is a parent, sibling, best friend, church leader, boss, coworker, or any number of people, you won't live up to what you think they expect. Maybe the expectations are realistic. We all need them. Most work-related positions have KPIs (key performance indicators) to know whether we are doing our job to the company's expectations. Those are required, but what doesn't work is when you take your position and compare it to someone else in the same place. You won't reason, decide, lead or look anything like him/her. So, begin to rest and be thankful for who you were created to be and the strengths you bring to every table you are called to sit at today.

What is your system? What is your calling? What is your greatest strength? I can hear you saying, "I don't have any; I was born without one." That is a lie because we are each uniquely gifted. The NLT Bible says (whether you believe or not), "*For God's gifts and His call can never be withdrawn.*" You were born with them. He destined them from the beginning of time. Maybe you just need to ask if you feel overlooked.

You have a piece of the worldwide puzzle. We all know how frustrating it is to be almost finished with a 2000-piece puzzle only to realize one or two pieces are missing. Bring your piece to the table. Step up to play. Maybe you have 1000, 100, 10, or only one piece; you are still just as valuable. Jesus said he would leave the 99 for the one. When we embrace our God-given identity, anything is possible.

Several years ago, when the selfie craze took off, I was very insecure and rarely took a picture. I couldn't even figure out how to do it. I must have snapped ten pictures to get the right one. You know how it goes: chin up, chin down, camera above, camera below, side shot, oops the wrong side, and then snap and you moved, and now it is blurry. Start the whole process again. AND THEN FILTERS appeared. Game changer, right? It is almost impossible to snap a bad selfie. I felt like a fraud, though. Because I knew if I ever went to a class reunion, they would be shocked at all the age lines that I have earned by growing old. I gave up the filter for the real me. Don't misunderstand, I love a good filter still and will never object when a friend wants to add one to our selfie, but I prefer to show people who I truly am, at least every other picture. A person with large front teeth, a long face, slightly oversized nose, age lines, a few gray hairs here and there before my six-week hair appointment, but a person I've grown to love because I was created in my Father's image.

Time to step out of the boat of sameness into the murky waters of adventure. Trust Him. He will guide you and take you places you've never thought possible as you begin to run your race. The thought of that may scare you. You might not want to travel, that is okay. He created you so He knows what you need, can do, can't do.

Do you struggle with organization? Do you want to be organized? My suggestion: call a professional like me and get a system installed in the garage, pantry, home office, and every closet in your home. I know you think this could be very costly. How much is your time worth? It is worth knowing that every time you need something, you know where it is? If we clocked how much time is spent looking for lost items, we would be surprised at our inefficiencies. My walk-in closet stays organized 24-7 because everything has a place.

I admit it. My parents were right. They tried to tell me, but it took time to understand. Don't get me wrong; my car often looks like a total wreck, stuff everywhere. Cars need to be designed by women. We would have a spot for everything: purses, key FOBs, coffee cups, kid's snacks, and we would not have a gap between the console and the chair. That gap becomes the void of all voids. Do they not realize it is hard to reach even my tiny hand into that area? Please car manufacturers; it is the 21st century. That space needs to be banned.

What about the fact that you are the first to say you can't make a decision? Why is that? We are all born decision-makers. Maybe you were raised with someone who made all your decisions for you, so you use that as an excuse for not making any. Cancel that thought. The decisions made on your behalf, whether bad or good, gave you the groundwork for making decisions. I anoint you a decision-maker. Practice makes perfect. Start small. When someone asks you where you want to eat, think about three things you want to eat, then throw out suggestions. My husband and I love to eat out. We are constantly asking one another where we want to go. I know that I will always eat a salad, so I offer several spots with a great salad offering when choosing. Most of the time, I get an eye roll because he knows my three faves.

For more significant decisions, much prayer is often needed. Although I must admit, I don't tarry long in indecision, which can negatively affect me. I may have needed to sit with an idea longer than I did, rather than jumping in headfirst only to find out I dove into the shallow end. As I sit here, I try to remember when I made a bad decision and wish I could go back. Honestly, I don't know of one that didn't teach me something, so I can't say I regret decisions made even in haste.

When my husband and I were buying our business, I had just left the corporate world, more of a forced exit due to the company closing its doors, and I definitely don't think I did my full due diligence. I was working as a consultant at the time when a franchise broker contacted me via LinkedIn. He saw that I was looking for work and had a "wonderful" franchise opportunity available for me. I deleted the message and moved on. I didn't want anything to do with owning a Subway. That was about the extent of my franchise knowledge. He contacted me again a month or so later, letting me know there are 100s of franchise opportunities available. It sparked my interest, but again I hit delete. Finally, he sent a message saying he would love to schedule a brief call to determine my eligibility as an entrepreneur based on personality and financial readiness. Now he was talking my language. You mean I could possibly buy a business that considered my personality? Yes, sign me up.

I called him, setting up a time to meet. He did do a personality and financial assessment and presented four franchises available for purchase. I didn't like any of them as soon as they were given. He had one more that he had reserved for the finale. He told us it would be at the peak of our financial competence. As he began explaining, everything within us shouted YES! My husband was even excited because he saw that we would bring our unique giftings to the table in this business. His propensity for all things operations and my love for people naturally gave us both a predisposition for sales.

We did a very basic due diligence research on our franchise, and within three months, we were signing on the dotted line. What normally takes people a year, we completed quickly. Looking back, I am still glad every day that we made the decision, but I would have removed the idealistic glasses that I had on during the vetting process. I had no comprehension of what was to come: managing a million widgets, employees, ever-changing schedules, client's needs, and finally, the bottom line. The responsibility has been more than I can bear at times, but

I am thankful I have a "silent" partner in Jesus. Actually, He is the ultimate owner, and my husband and I are the stewards. He has gotten us out of so many pickles over the years.

One small example of how Jesus is the Human Resource Director Supreme is when He saved the day a few years back. I was at a local coffee shop training a new sales designer, mid-afternoon. My phone rang, and my husband sounded frustrated regarding an install that was going perfectly until the client saw the handles on her garage cabinet doors and freaked out. I could hear her yelling in the background that I gave her the wrong handles. Kalani put her on the phone, and there was no talking to her. She was irate. I tried to explain that other handles had never been discussed. She insisted that I promised her another kind. I told her that I would have displayed them in the design if I had promised another kind.

I am sure you are thinking: just change the handles; how hard can that be? This client had chosen our most high-end door (very pricey), and the handles drilled were nothing like the handles she wanted, which would have required ordering new doors. I had a decision to make? Give in or go to prayer. I told Kalani I was hanging up and would pray that God intervenes. Not ten minutes later, he called back to tell me all was settled. He said to her that the handles she thought she was getting would be sharp and difficult to use when opening the doors. She agreed and was happy with the ones already installed. I must admit that those ten minutes were grueling. I paced and prayed outside that coffee shop that day, but He came through as He is the ultimate Customer Relations Director. You see, He loves the unhappy client and the unhappy business owner all at the same time.

Since purchasing a business, I've often been reminded of a story in 1 Kings 3:16-28 about Solomon's wisdom when deciding who the mother of a child was. The gist of the story is that two women came before King Solomon, the first one pleading the King to give her child back because woman number 2 had stolen him. Both women were prostitutes living in the same house, and both had newborn babies. One woman's child died, and, in the night, she placed her dead child in the arms of the other woman and took the other's woman's child as her own. Both sounded convincing before Solomon. In his wisdom, he asked for a sword to divide the baby, knowing that the real mom would stand up and say, "No, give him to her." And it happened exactly like that, and the real mom went home with her baby.

Hebrews 13:8 in NLT says, "*Jesus Christ is the same yesterday, today and forever.*" I have access to the wisdom of Solomon. I need to ask. Over the past seven years, I've asked more than my fair share, and He has been faithful every time. Sometimes the answer is different than I want to hear, but it is a perfect answer nonetheless.

I am reminded of a *hot mess* moment in my prior career, which needed the wisdom of Solomon. I was working as a Team Lead, managing ten employees who were investigators for a private contractor doing background checks on those requiring a security clearance. One of my investigators called me in a panic, letting me know she'd lost her credentials, which was an immediate suspension call, which always led to a dismissal. She said she looked everywhere. Not only was she my employee but a dear friend from church. I knew I needed to report it because our credentials were a federal law enforcement badge, and In the wrong hands, it could be detrimental. Before I raised the flag of concern with upper management, I stopped and prayed. Supernaturally I could see where they were in her company car.

I told her to hold tight, I would be at her house shortly. I drove over and proceeded to look. She insisted she'd done all that. As I was feeling around under the passenger seat, I felt a strange black box that houses the electronic equipment to move the seat forward and back. I lifted it slightly, and right there were the credentials lodged in the black box. They were almost unseen because the badge was the same color as the box and the carpet. It all blended in. Had we not prayed, nor asked, we would have thought all was lost. "*Ask, and you shall receive.*" Even in the smallest of things, IT ALL MATTERS TO HIM.

Hopefully, this book has equipped you with the knowledge that if we first partner with Christ, knowing we've been given the "*mind of Christ,*" "*we can do all things through Christ who strengthens us.*" What are you saying to yourself daily?

- I don't have gifts/talents. I am not smart enough.

- I was born into the wrong family.

- You don't know my past. You had it better than me.

All excuses. Again, "*Ask, and you shall receive.*" I've said it many times throughout the book; there is no one like you on the planet, so stop comparing yourself to someone else. Jesus is the only one who should be on the other end of our yardstick. Why? Because He is perfect, He paid the ultimate price for each one of us, and He loves us unconditionally.

Yet, there is more. I may have *hot mess* moments, but I will never consider myself a hot mess. I've been reformed. I am focused, and even when not, I am made whole.

Phase 12

Not Mess — the Rest of the Story

What else is there to tell? So much more. I have the following books in my heart that need to be written:

- Hot Mess to Not Mess in my Marriage

- Hot Mess to Not Mess in my Relationships

- Hot Mess to Not Mess in my Finances

The next book will start from the beginning. I've given you a sneak peek at my early life, but there is so much more to say. I will introduce my family's matriarch (with her permission) and the decisions she made and those made for her that changed the course of not only her life but mine. We all have that story. Funny, we often think our decisions are our own without one thought of the consequences, whether good or bad, that they will have on others. We live in a world that says, "Make your own independent decisions as long as they feel good for you." I wish that were true, but it is so far from reality.

My next book will be challenging as it involves heartbreak, drugs, sexual indiscretion, and abuse while not realizing its effects on the next generation. The redemption story is even more powerful than the heartbreak. I cannot begin to describe how God steps in and rewrites our history even when it seems like nothing will change. He is gracious, and He loves us. There are times when I wish He were in a greater hurry to see a transformation, but His timing is perfect!

We've all got a story to tell. I am thankful that you've been here to read parts of mine. I am a recovering mess, working daily with Jesus. "He never leaves me nor forsakes me." Even when those around me can't love me the way I need love, He reminds me that He can. I no longer put my hope in the need for other's approval. And when I do, I find myself doing an about-face back to the only One whose approval counts. There I am never disappointed, never have unmet expectations, and never feel unloved. His promises are true, so I stand on them as a reminder of who I am.

Be on the lookout for the next book as we travel back to the past, well, really the future, Lord willing, at the end of 2021.

If you read this book and had no clue about the person of Jesus, I want to invite you to make Him the Lord of your life. To walk with Him, allowing Him to meet you in all your vulnerabilities. A simple prayer will do. Repeat after me. "Jesus, I've lived without you for far too long. I want to take part in the great exchange. I repent of my sins, Jesus, and ask you to be the Lord and Savior of my life. Thank you for forgiving my sins, paying the price on the cross. I receive you today."

If you prayed that prayer, please message me on FB under my professional page: Dana Reed Nuesca. I will respond and rejoice with you. You've truly made the best decision you will ever make.

With all that said, there's even more to share! So, I'll end with this... to be continued.

Acknowledgements:

To all those who took the time to read my book, scouring the pages for incorrect content that didn't make sense: my Dad, Marsha Wooten, Rowena Hatten, Elaine Welty, Kara Horat, and Lori Clifton.

To Marcy Browe Photography for capturing so many wonderful photos for my brand, and for the amazing cover shot for this book. Your talent and eye for detail make all your work spectacular.

About the Author:

Dana (rhymes with banana) Reed Nuesca is a 5th generation Californian and Maui transplant at the age of 11. She married her high school sweetheart three weeks before her 19th birthday, had one child at the age of 20, and now has five grandkids (three biological and two chosen by God). She resides in North County, San Diego, until the Lord says otherwise. She has a Bachelor's degree in Communications with a minor in English and a Master's degree in Management. She also co-founded Seeds of Hope International in 2012, which now serves the needs of others in five countries. Her most outstanding achievement is saying "YES" to Jesus when He called! He has changed her life for eternity, and she knows He will do the same for you.

Connect with Dana Reed Nuesca on Facebook and Instagram @DanaReedNuesca.

Endnotes:

Links:

1 Samantha Lauriello | May 7 2019 | A Psychologist Explains Why People Gossip—and the Reason Might Surprise You | Explore Health, Mind Body | https://www.health.com/mind-body/why-do-people-gossip

2 Urban Dictionary | Shart Definition | https://www.urbandictionary.com/define.php?term=shar t

3 Lori Clifton | Book | Transformed: The Journey from Despair to Extreme Hope |

4 https://www.psycom.net/what-is-trichotillomania/